Coding with Basher ™

CODE YOUR OWN WEBSITE

Coding with Basher ™

CODE YOUR OWN WEBSITE

KINGFISHER
LONDON & NEW YORK

KINGFISHER
LONDON & NEW YORK

Text and design copyright © Toucan Books Ltd 2019
Illustrations copyright © Simon Basher 2019
www.basherbooks.com

Published in the United States by Kingfisher
175 Fifth Ave., New York, NY 10010
Kingfisher is an imprint of Macmillan Children's Books, London

Author: theCoderSchool
Consultants: Robin Ulster and James Denby
Editor: Anna Southgate
Designer: Leah Germann
Indexer: Marie Lorimer

Dedicated to Nathan Beasley

Distributed in the U.S. and Canada by Macmillan,
175 Fifth Ave., New York, NY 10010

Library of Congress Cataloging-in-Publication Data
has been applied for

ISBN 978-0-7534-7511-9 (Hardcover)
ISBN 978-0-7534-7512-6 (Paperback)

Kingfisher books are available for special promotions and premiums.
For details contact: Special Markets Department, Macmillan,
175 Fifth Ave., New York, NY 10010.

For more information, please visit www.kingfisherbooks.com

Printed in China

9 8 7 6 5 4 3 2 1
1TR/0519/WKT/UG/128MA

CONTENTS

INTRODUCTION

Hey there, are you ready to code? While coding is used in all technology, this book focuses on website coding found on the Internet. Starting with a look at the Internet itself, you'll get to know all the characters that play a role. Of course, you'll meet Browser and Website, and will also hear from Basic Server, Router, and URL, among others. Then, after briefly hanging out with the folks from Online Safety and Website Tools, you'll meet three major coding languages: HTML, CSS, and JavaScript. Hot on their heels comes Dynamic Server and *then* you get to code your very own dynamic website using some advanced friends like PHP. Wow! That's quite a journey, so let's get started.

Why Code?

Coding, or computer programming, isn't just for engineers, it's for everyone! Whether you grow up to be a doctor, lawyer, artist, athlete, (or coder!), you can bet technology will be a big part of your professional (and personal) life. Knowing how to code will help you understand technology. It will also let you practice thinking in a logical, structured way—a crucial skill for all activities. So get coding—long gone are the days when coding was only for nerds. (Plus, nerds are cool!)

What's theCoderSchool?

theCoderSchool is a cool and fun place for kids to learn how to code. Founded in 2014 and based smack in the heart of Silicon Valley, California, the school is growing fast with locations around the country. Its founders Hansel and Wayne wrote this book and they are honored to be sharing their experiences with you. You can find out more about them online, at www.thecoderschool.com.

THE INTERNET

You've probably heard of me. Also known as The Cloud, I am the world's most global network! A long time ago, I started out as a small military project called ARPANET, but now I'm connected to almost everything you can imagine, from your cell phone to your tablet and computers all around the world. Soon, I'll hook up with the refrigerator in your kitchen and cars on the streets, too. Connect to me, and I'll have you talking to people and computers everywhere in an instant!

ARPANET

Not many people have heard of me, but I am the Internet's big brother. I started out in the 1960s, as a way of connecting computers nearby and letting them talk to each other.

I was dreamed up by DARPA, an agency launched by the U.S. military that wanted to find new technologies for keeping the United States safe. The agency explored the idea of linking computers to one another, thinking it could help improve military communications. Eventually they created a network called ARPANET—that's me!

I sent my very first message in 1969 from Los Angeles to Palo Alto, a suburb of San Francisco and the birthplace of Silicon Valley. The message read "login," but only the first two letters made it before the system crashed! No worries, I soon got over that little disaster and, within no time, everybody was using me.

1

Plain Talking

- **DARPA:** Defense Advanced Research Projects Agency
- **ARPANET:** Advanced Research Projects Agency Network
- **SURF THE INTERNET:** To spend time visiting a lot of websites.

In the Know:

The World Wide Web was invented by Tim Berners-Lee in the late 1980s. It's the segment of the Internet that browsers use to show web pages to people. Everything that has a "www." prefix is part of that web.

Go Figure!

Once the World Wide Web was invented, any computer with a browser could get online and surf the Internet. From 1995 to now, the number of users has risen from 16 million to over 4 billion. That's more than half of the world's population! Today, half of the traffic on the Internet is from cell phones.

INTERNET BASICS

The Internet sure is complicated—it's got lots of gizmos and technological magic that make it run. Take out the complex stuff, and you'll find me, a much simpler way to explain how the Internet works.

The Internet is made up of a world of computers all sharing information with each other and all "following protocol" to talk in pretty much the same way. I have three basic parts: a requester (a.k.a. the client), the network, and a responder (a.k.a. Server). For example, all World Wide Web traffic starts with a request from a browser client. That request travels through the Internet network to Server, which sends back a response. Take a look at pages 28–29 to see how it all works.

Take a look at pages 28–29 to see how it all works.

Plain Talking

- **PROTOCOL:** The rules, procedures, and formats for sending data from one device to another.

- **CLIENT:** Another name for a computer when it makes a request, such as wanting to look at a website.

In the Know:

The Internet sends a client's request to the right server and gets a response back from that server to the client. In most cases, this happens by bouncing the information through a chain of computers and routers in a few blinks of an eye.

Following Protocol

Imagine the millions of requests and responses that get sent daily between computers. Now picture the many computers and routers involved in passing all of that data through the Internet. To make things run smoothly, all computers need to follow the same set of rules, procedures, and formats. These are called "network protocols" and they allow computers to talk to each other using the same "language."

WEBSITE

Look at me! I'm the center of attention, the very thing that most people look for on the Internet! Think Amazon, Google, and YouTube: me, me, and me!

I'm made up of web pages that are created using three programming languages: HTML, CSS, and JavaScript. You simply click here or there when you want to go to a new page—Link will tell you how it works. I am used for all kinds of things: shopping, doing homework, watching movies, ordering takeout. The possibilities are practically endless. Search engines Google and Bing (also me!) will help you find what you are looking for. Almost every business or organization has a website, as does every school. In short, if you need to find out about something—anything—you're more than likely to find it online, using me!

In the Know:

Many people use website and web page interchangeably, but they are two different things. A website is made up of a collection of web pages. So, you might surf to the Amazon web*site*, and click around to look at various products on different web *pages*, all of which are part of the Amazon website.

View Source

Open up any website from your browser—say, www.google.com. Right-click (Ctrl-click on a Mac) near a blank part of the website, and find the menu item that says "View Source." Wow, looks complicated, right?! Everything in there is either HTML, CSS, or JavaScript. Many websites have code that not only shows you something, but performs other tasks, such as tracking your login and showing ads.

URL

1

Plain Talking

- **HTTP:** HyperText Transfer Protocol, the rules used by the World Wide Web.

- **HTTPS:** Adding an "s" means a protocol is secure, so that hackers are less able to steal information.

I'm known by my initials: U-R-L. Please say that you've heard of me already? No? Well, my letters stand for Uniform Resource Locator, but I am often referred to as "web address," which is probably easier to understand. That's me, you see, an address for a destination on the World Wide Web, such as a website or a web page. When you type me in, you are making a request to be taken to a specific place that can only be identified by me. The standard URL format includes things like protocol, domain, and (obviously) web page.

In the Know:

URLs are most commonly used to get to a web page, but they can also direct you to images, files, or any other resource. We also use them to help navigate around the web by linking to other web pages.

DOMAIN

Knock-knock! Hello? Anybody there? I'm the place that Website likes to call home. I come right at the end of Website's main address. You've heard of google.com and disney.com? Well, these are all "top-level" versions of me—that is, the main domain for any business, service, or organization.

Most of the time, my name ends in ".com," but sometimes you'll see my last part as ".org," ".io," or any number of other endings, all separated by a period. Type my name into Browser, and you'll get taken to Website. It's as easy as that!

In the Know:

The first registered .com domain was created by a now extinct computer manufacturer called Symbolics Inc. It was called www. symbolics.com (no surprises there), and was created on March 15, 1985. Just over 30 years later, there are close to 300 million domains today.

1

BROWSER

1

You know me! I'm the handy tool that allows you to "browse" the Internet. My many versions include Chrome, Firefox, Safari, and Edge. I generate all Internet requests for the World Wide Web. Not only that, but when a response comes through, it's my job to interpret Server's code and display it in a way that you can understand. So that I can read the responses, Server has to send them using HTML code, usually with a little CSS and JavaScript thrown in for good measure. You'll get to know that programming trio better later on.

TRY THIS!

Log on to any browser and look for the following buttons or bars. All browsers have these same features in common:

- Address bar
- Home
- Back/Forward
- Refresh/Reload
- Stop

In the Know:

Originally, browsers didn't have images, just text. Now they look snazzy with lots of bells and whistles. Today you can browse the Internet from almost any device—computer, cell phone, or tablet, even some cars and TVs.

BASIC SERVER

Remember all those requests and responses Internet Basics talked about? Well, I'm the one responsible for sending back all the responses (*response*-ible, geddit?).

There are millions of me all over the world, all connected to the Internet. I'm super busy 24/7 responding to all the requests from client computers for things like websites. I package up data and send it back for browsers to read. Later on, Dynamic Server will explain how server code can be used to tailor the pages I send back to the requester, to give the very latest information.

Plain Talking

- **BROWSER CODE:**
  A.k.a. the "front end," browser code deals with elements for the user, such as what the web page looks like and the popups they see.

- **SERVER CODE:**
  A.k.a. the "back end," server code takes care of things that a computer needs to remember: logins, passwords, or the latest data updates.

1

ROUTER

Ha! The Internet! That guy would be lost without me! It's true that the Internet has great connections, but I'm the one who makes sure all those connections hook up with the right destinations.

Think about the millions of post offices in the world, and how each one is part of a bigger network making sure every single letter is delivered to the correct address. That's exactly how I operate—me and my other router pals, that is. The difference is that everything we send via the Internet is known collectively as "traffic" and not "mail."

You've heard Internet Basics talking about requests and responses? Well, I join up with other routers to pass data packets through different networks until Browser's request is routed to the correct destination server. Then we repeat the same process to return the response back to Browser.

1

Plain Talking

- **DATA PACKET:** All data is split into small chunks, or packets. Each travels separately to its destination and the original message is reassembled on arrival.

- **WI-FI**: A networking technology that allows devices to communicate wirelessly.

In the Know:

Internet traffic includes everything from communicating with businesses, friends, and family to streaming media from entertainment sites, and from sharing files with others to searching for information.

Home Routers

Most people have a router in their home these days. Modern home routers receive data from computers and other devices using Wi-Fi technology. They then route it to the home's modem. It's then the modem's job to send that data out to the Internet via your Internet Service Provider (ISP). Typically, it does this using a phone line or a cable line.

INTERNET SERVICE PROVIDER

Want to get onto the Internet? Sorry, but there is only one way to do this, and that's by using me! Internet Service Provider—that's a long name, right, so people call me ISP for short (not "isp," as in wisp, but I-S-P). Think of me as a gatekeeper. Your home computer has to contact me when you want to get onto the Internet!

I'm any organization that provides services for accessing, using, or participating in the Internet. Your home devices usually connect to a modem in your home, which then sends data to my computers so that I can figure out where your request should go. Big names like AT&T or Xfinity are some of the ISPs you might have heard of.

In the Know:

Internet Service Providers came about in Australia and the United States when folks first started using the Internet in the late 1980s. One of the first ISP companies was called AOL and it used telephone lines to get users onto the Internet. Ask an adult if they remember the fancy beep-and-buzz sounds of the first dial-up modems.

All about the Modem

Internet Service Providers can connect your home to the Internet in a number of ways, most commonly using telephone lines, cable lines, or even fiber-optic lines and satellites. If you have Internet access at home, there is probably one of these kinds of connections hooking you up!

1

DNS SERVER

Have you ever seen a phone book full of business addresses and their telephone numbers? I'm like one of those and will look up any website address you care to give me. Because computers don't have addresses that people can easily read, and because it's hard for people to remember lots of numbers, I was created to help translate!

The Domain Name System (DNS) is the naming system that associates a name with a computer's address. As the DNS Server, I work with my buddy Internet Service Provider to translate Website's proper name into an address that computers understand. It's called an IP Address and is made up of lots of numbers. This tells you where the computer is that holds the website you are looking for. Without me, you'd have to remember all of those numbers to get to Website—so you're welcome!

1

Plain Talking

- **DOMAIN NAME SYSTEM:** The system that knows which name goes with which computer.

- **IP ADDRESS:** A string of numbers like 123.45.6.78 that a computer uses to identify itself.

In the Know:

DNS servers do not reside in your home or on your computer. Instead, your ISP provides access to a DNS server for you. When you make a request, it is this DNS server that performs the translation from the website's domain name to the computer's IP address.

A Numbers Game

Nowadays there are so many computers using the Internet that we're running out of numbers for IP Addresses! Another format has emerged to help deal with this, called IPv6 (Internet Protocol version 6). An IPv6 address might look like this:

2001:0db8:85a3:0000:0000:8a2e:0370:7334.

THE CLOUD

Hello down there! The view from up here is amazing! I am The Cloud, a.k.a. the Internet, but I was just kidding about the view! When people refer to me, they're not actually talking about anything white and fluffy and up in the sky, but rather the (big!) group of computers, routers, and other devices on the Internet. They called me The Cloud because, just like a real cloud, I have no set form since computers are constantly joining and leaving the group. People have used other names to describe me in the past, such as The Web, Cyberspace, and The Information Superhighway.

Beyond being a handy metaphor, I offer a neat range of "cloud services," that run and save information on the Internet instead of just on your computer.

Plain Talking

- **PRIMARY NETWORK:** A network that is strategically placed around the world to help speed up communication time across the globe.

In the Know:

The Cloud has a "backbone." This is the name given to the physical connections between the Internet's primary networks. An example of this is the network of big underwater fiber-optic pipes that connect computers residing on both sides of the world's largest oceans.

Cloud vs. Local Services

A "cloud" service is something that runs on the Internet, accessible from any computer with a browser after logging in. Examples include YouTube or Google Docs. A "local" service is something that sits only on a standalone device. For example, if you film and watch a video on your phone, that's local. You need that phone to watch it, and can't access it from anywhere else. Cloud Services are great because you can use them with almost any Internet-connected device, and the information isn't lost if your computer is broken.

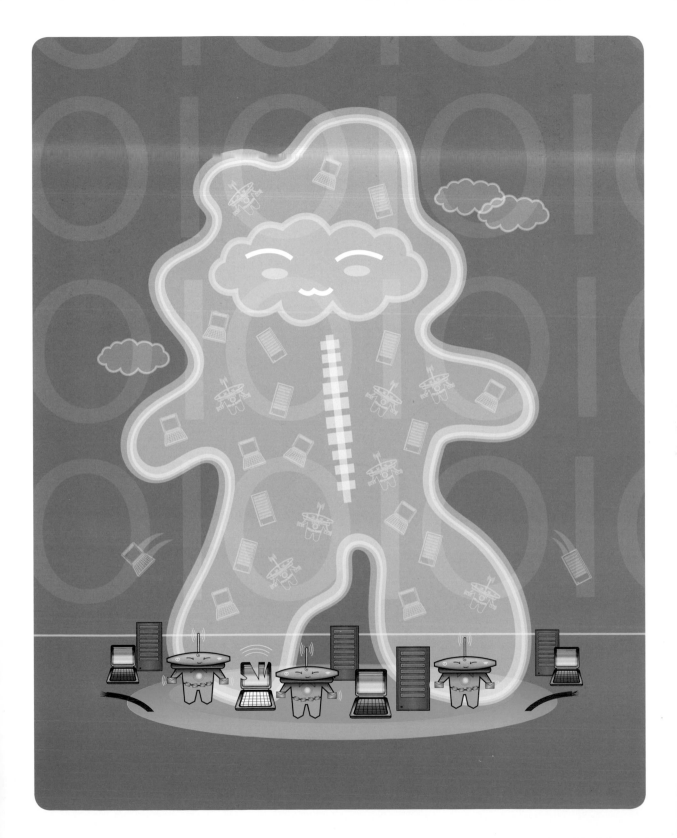

THE INTERNET IN ACTION

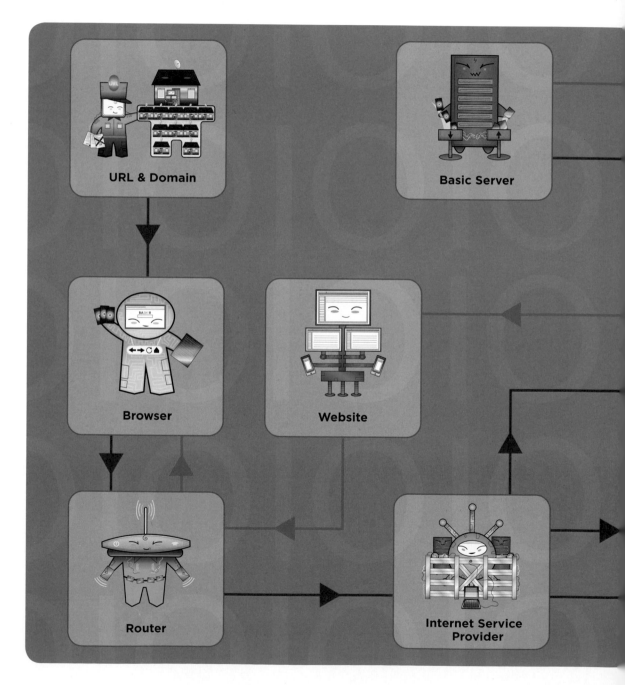

URL & Domain

Basic Server

Browser

Website

Router

Internet Service Provider

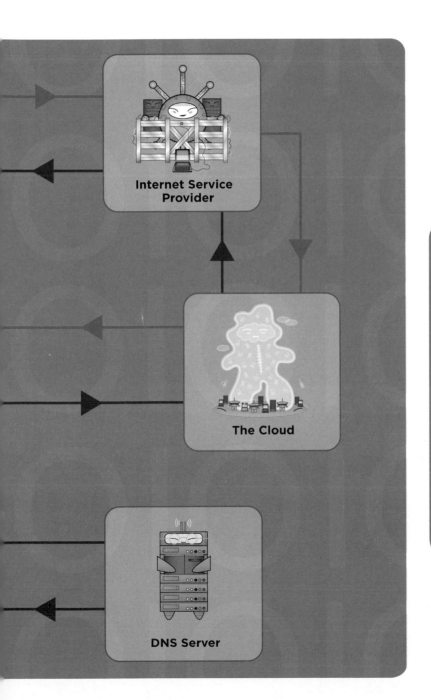

Internet Service Provider

The Cloud

DNS Server

In the Know:

Now that you have met the Internet crew, you can see how they all work so well together. Follow the red arrows to see what happens when Browser sends out a request for Website. Once Server receives the request, you can use the blue arrows to trace the path taken by Server's response.

▶ Browser request

▶ Server response

ONLINE SAFETY

The Internet is like a giant ocean. It's filled with all kinds of weird and wonderful things (check out Social Media), but there are a few troublemakers out there, too. I'm talking about the mean types who like to hide behind the anonymity of the Internet—Cyberbully and Online Bad Guy. Read on, and you'll learn all about them. Don't worry, these nasties can be avoided if you know how, and I'm here to help. My friend Privacy will show you how to stay safe.

CYBERBULLY

2

DO IT NOW!

If you are being bullied, talk to an adult you trust. Ask them to block the number or user ID of a bully so you can't see his or her messages. Report the cyberbully so they can be investigated, and keep any evidence that could be useful.

In the Know:

Cyberbullying includes: Sending nasty messages by text, email, or on social media; posting embarrassing news about someone, without permission; repeatedly hassling someone while playing online games; and pretending to be someone else to get what you want.

Everyone knows about bullies. I use technology—a phone, a computer, or even an Xbox—to taunt my victims. I can send mean text messages or emails, I can spread a nasty rumor on a social networking site, or I can post embarrassing photos and videos. All I need is a device that others connect to. You could say that I am more cowardly than a normal bully because I hide behind my computer. It means I can play real dirty by encouraging others to gang up on you or by posting my messages anonymously, so you don't even know who I am.

ONLINE BAD GUY

I'm the kind of baddie that uses lies to persuade kids to be my friends. It's so easy! I hang out with Social Media, waiting for someone like you to come along. I'm sneaky, smart, and learn about the latest trends so that I can talk to you about kids' stuff. I might be an adult, but can pretend to be anyone online. I'll get you to share personal details, send pictures, and even meet me in the real world. Be very wary of me, because these are risks you don't want to take.

DO IT NOW!

Take precautions to avoid online bad guys:

- Use privacy settings to reduce the amount of personal information you share online.

- Only interact with people you know in real life.

- Never arrange to meet anyone you don't know personally.

- If something doesn't feel right, talk to a trusted adult about it and get help.

SOCIAL MEDIA

Hey there! How are you doing? Come and have a chat with me. Can't you tell that I am very friendly? It's just in my nature to be social. I say the best way to make friends is by being a good sharer and I'm probably the best in the world. Just look at the different forms I take. I can be a blog, a business network, a social network, a forum, or a microblog. Or perhaps you'll find me photo or video sharing. I'm also into social gaming and taking a trip or two in a virtual world. Come and join me!

Take care, though. By being so friendly and sharing, I also have to know exactly who I'm interacting with, since I don't want to run into Cyberbully and Online Bad Guy. My motto is simple: "If in doubt, don't share." Make sure you remember that, too.

Plain Talking

- **GOING VIRAL:** Things go viral when something being shared is so interesting that everyone who reads it sends it on to others. It just keeps getting shared over and over again.

DO IT NOW!

Make sure you have good privacy settings if you plan on sharing personal information. You don't want to share everything with everyone. The more personal the information you want to share, the more privacy rules you need.

Social Whirl

Most people agree that Six Degrees, founded in 1996, was the first social networking website. Many others, such as Friendster and MySpace, have tried and failed. Ask an older friend or relative if they ever had an account on one of these sites. Nowadays, top social media websites include Facebook, YouTube, Twitter, and Instagram. Who knows if the popular social media sites we use today will still be here in the future?

PRIVACY

Howdy partner! I consider myself the sheriff of the Internet—I am here to help protect its users. Imagine how violated you would feel if information that you had no intention of sharing with others became public. Well, it's my job to help you protect your information and keep it private.

Whenever you are connected to the Internet by cell phone, tablet, or computer, be sure to check your privacy settings. These include things like other computers needing to ask you before accessing your location, or whether to allow cookies on your device. Depending on your comfort level, you can adjust the settings to be more or less restrictive. In doing so, you will be using your privacy settings to protect your PII.

Plain Talking

- **PII:** Personal Identifying Information. This includes such things as your full name, email address, home address, social security #, passport #, birth date/place.

- **IDENTITY THEFT:** When a criminal gets hold of your PII and uses it to act like you and make purchases or borrow money, leaving you stuck with the bill.

Gone Phishing

A common Internet scam is called "phishing." This is where a criminal sets up a fake web page—a login page resembling one for a service you use, for example. When you enter your login details, the criminal steals your information and uses it to gain access to your account.

WEBSITE TOOLS

If you are going to build a website, you'll want to get to know my crew! These folks can turn an idea in your mind into a real website on the World Wide Web. As with all technology, the tools used to make and run websites are changing constantly—with new parts added and old ones retired. Established tools get easier to use and brand-new tools come into play. There may be new ways of doing things, but the basics rarely change, so let's discover what they are all about!

WEBSITE BUILDER

There are many ways to build your own website, but I am by far the easiest. Go down the difficult route and you will find yourself writing a lot of code. Pick me, though, and you have an instant shortcut!

You see, I'm a tool that lets you decide how you want your website to look, and I automatically create the code for you. Better still, most versions of me allow you to choose your domain, and will even host your code too. I'm like a one-stop shop! Most website builders come with different templates you can choose to try new looks easily. They even come with a set of cool images you can use for an instantly amazing-looking website!

Plain Talking

- **RESPONSIVE WEBSITE:** A website that looks good on a cell phone as well as on a computer. Half of all Internet traffic is from a cell phone. Quite difficult to code, this is something many website builders can help with.

TRY THIS!

Search online for "best website builder" and you're bound to find funny names like Wix or Weebly. They're very easy to use. Sign up for a free account, follow the directions, and you could have a beautiful website in no time!

Going the Extra Mile

Working with a website builder can help you build a website quickly, but this tool has its limits. In order to create a website that has lots of functions, learn to code it yourself using HTML, CSS, and JavaScript.

3

DOMAIN NAME REGISTRAR

3

I'm Domain's traffic cop, helping to direct Internet requests to your website's code on your server. I let you choose, buy, and own your domain, and make sure that whatever cool-sounding domain name you want isn't already being used elsewhere in the world. Doubling up as DNS Server, I also hold the key to where your website is located. If your website ever changes location, I'm the first one you tell about it and it's me that tells everyone else!

DNS Propagation

There are many domain name registrars around the world. All DNS servers know the IP addresses of all websites. If an address changes, the domain name registrar sends an update. This process is called DNS Propagation.

In the Know:

Domain name registrars work with an organization called ICANN (Internet Corporation for Assigned Names and Numbers). This worldwide, nonprofit company holds the complete list of domain names. It coordinates with the domain name registrars to make sure each name is unique.

WEBSITE HOST

Feel the Heat

Computers give off a lot of heat. In 2018, Microsoft put a server farm at the bottom of the ocean just off the coast of Scotland to help regulate the temperature!

3

My pal Website is made up of lots of computer code and it all has to sit somewhere—with me in fact! Think of me as a big old box happily storing all the goodies that make Website so amazing—code, pictures, files, you name it. When you type Website's URL into Browser, the Internet uses ISP and DNS Server to come to me for Website's code.

For advanced websites—the kind where data changes daily—I also hold Server Code, which creates pages on the fly!

In the Know:

To build a website from scratch, you need to register your domain, and find a host. Many online tools offer the whole package.

CODE PLAYGROUND

Ever feel like you want to run some code without having to deal with Domain Name Registrar and Website Host? Well, come to me! Just as my name implies, I'm a playground, a place where you can experiment and quickly see the results. I'm a free online tool that lets you write all three kinds of website code (HTML, CSS, and JavaScript—you'll meet these guys later) and combine it to see the results right away. For example, you might try out some single CSS or JavaScript commands just to see how they run outside of a full development setup. You can even create an account and save your code for later. Developers use me all the time before going live with their code.

3

TRY THIS!

To see a good example of a playground, type **jsfiddle.net** into your browser.

In the area labeled "HTML," type in **"<h1>Hello World </h1>"** (notice how it created an ending </h1> tag for you). Press **Run** in the menu. You just ran some HTML in a browser!

In the Know:

All code playgrounds have a results area. This shows what your webpage would look like if you combined all three of the languages into one file and gave it to a browser to read. Turn to Chapter 8 to see how to take the code you write using a code playground and put it onto a real website for everyone to see.

Language Savvy

Code playgrounds typically support HTML, CSS, and JavaScript. Many allow you to experiment with other languages, too—more than 100 languages in some cases! The goal is always the same. It's simply a way to experiment with short bits of code.

HTML

One of a trio of browser languages, I am the basic building block of everything on the World Wide Web! My full name is HyperText Markup Language, but everybody calls me HTML. I use a series of tags to tell Browser what goes in Website. Unlike most coding languages, I'm not very logical. In other words, you can't use variables, loops, or any of the other things most languages can do. My job is simply to tell Browser Website's content—that's it!

TAG AND ATTRIBUTE

HTML consists mostly of us—two nifty ways of marking (literally "tagging") Website's content. Whenever you see code within angled brackets, < and >, you're looking at Tag. Tag comes in pairs, with an opening tag and a closing tag to identify the content in between—for example, <h1>Hi!</h1>.

Sometimes Attribute sits inside the opening Tag to give Browser a little more information. Usually, Attribute looks like a name=value pair, like "id=myfirstheader" below. Older versions of HTML used attributes often, but nowadays many attributes have moved to CSS—check that guy out to see how it works.

TRY THIS!

Consider the following code:

```
<h1 id=myfirstheader>Hello World</h1>
```

| beginning tag | attribute | content | ending tag |

This tells the browser that the words "Hello World" should appear in h1 (Header 1) style. The attribute says more about the header. The browser won't print the <h1> tag, but prints any content between the tags in Header 1 style, which is usually large and bold. Try typing it in yourself in JSFiddle.

4

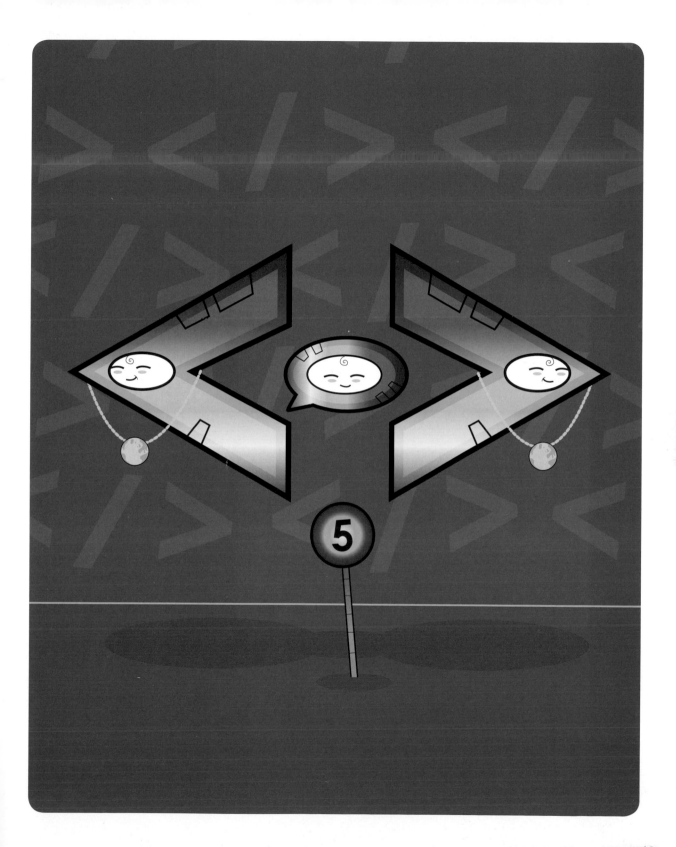

HTML STRUCTURE

A stickler for organization, I like a web page to follow my format. For example, the very first line of code should be a "doctype declaration" that looks exactly like this: <!DOCTYPE html>. It is followed by <html>, which tells Browser to expect an HTML document. Next comes the <head>, which tells Browser more about the content of the web page. Obviously, after <head> comes <body>. This is the part of the document that contains all the good stuff that will show up on the web page—words, images, video— each one coded with Tag and Attribute.

4

TRY THIS!

Here's a basic example of how an HTML document should be structured.

<!DOCTYPE html>	Declares this to be an HTML document.
<html>	Also declares this to be an HTML document.
<head>	Start of the header.
<title>My First Web Page Title</title>	Title that shows on a browser's tab.
<meta name="description" content="Really cool content about my website">	A description for search engines such as Google to know what the website is about.
</head>	End of the header.
<body>	Start of your content.
<h1 id=myfirstheader>Hello World</h1>	Our sample content.
</body>	End of your content.
</html>	End of document.

FORMATTING TAG

TRY THIS!

Try this code in the HTML window of JSFiddle:

<h1>This is a heading!</h1>

**<p>This paragraph has a <b>bold</b> word and a
line break.</p>**

In the Know:

HTML ignores multiple spaces and when you hit enter/return and go to the next line. Try adding them to your code in JSFiddle, and you'll see they don't show in the results. Instead use <p> or <br> to format your code.

I'm an HTML tag in bookish mode—I help make a web page easy to read. I'm a cousin to the more powerful CSS properties you'll learn about later, and help style text to make a web page look like the pages of a book.

For a long document, I have heading styles <h1> to <h6>. With <p>, I set the spacing you need between paragraphs. And for a smaller line break, I have <br>. My other formatting options include <b>bold</b>, <i>italics</i>, and many, many more.

IMAGE AND LINK

TRY THIS!

Try using the <a> and <img> tags in JSFiddle:

**<p>Here's a link to <a href="https://www.google.com">Google</a>, and an image on the next line:
<img src="https://server.thecoderschool.com/images/tcs.png">.**

In the Know:

Try this shortcut for typing a long image URL. Find an image you like on the Internet, hover your mouse over it, and right-click (ctrl-click on a Mac). Choose the option that says "Copy Image Address." You can then paste that address in place of the image URL in the example above.

4

The Internet would be a dull place without us: No pictures to look at and no means of getting from one place to another. But *with* us, it's another story. You see, Image gives Website more personality, and with just one click on some blue underlined text, Link can really take you places! Just imagine what happens when we work as a team! Of course, we can't take all the credit for our work, but rely on the services of Tag and Attribute to help us do our magic.

TABLE TAG

I'm an HTML tag in chart mode. You see, I've got this thing for alignment and I'm just not going to let it go! It's my job to help line up the text and images on a web page so everything looks like a nicely charted table of information. Without me, a web page would look all scattered about.

I just love to show lots of information in a matrix—say, a table of student names and the schools they attend. I have three main tags, stacked within each other—my <table> tag defines the whole table. Within that tag are <tr> tags. These define the rows in the table. Within the <tr> tags are <td> tags, and these define the cells. Sometimes cells are actually headings in the table—in that case, I use my heading tag, <th>!

4

TRY THIS!

Try this code in the HTML window of JSFiddle:

<table>

<tr>

<th>Student</th>

<th>School</th>

</tr>

<tr>

<td>Sally Jones</td>

<td>East Elementary</td>

</tr>

<tr>

<td>John Smith</td>

<td>North High School</td>

</table>

Remember, the spacing in the code doesn't matter, it's for readability only!

Student	School
Sally Jones	East Elementary
John Smith	North High School

When to Use Table Tags

HTML tables can help line up data, but it's not always the best tag to use to format information. Advanced developers use <div> tags with CSS for aligning things on a page, like centering pictures or lining up paragraphs of text on the page.

iFRAME

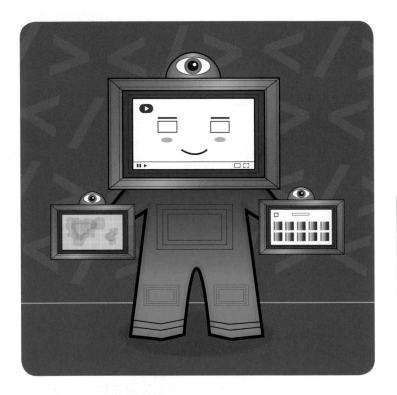

One of the coolest aspects of coding is being able to share and reuse stuff, and it's my job to help you do it! If you've seen YouTube videos inside other websites you are pretty much looking at me: an embedded iFrame! Lots of companies build really cool stuff that you can easily reuse and include on your own website. Things you might be able to embed include Google maps, a social media sharer, and even a whole website!

TRY THIS!

Most websites that let you embed their tools give you the code to copy and paste. Here's how you'd do it for YouTube:

- Find a favorite video.

- Click the "Share" button below the video.

- Choose the "Embed" option, and you should be shown HTML code that starts with <iframe> and ends with </iframe>.

- Click on "Copy."

- In JSFiddle, paste the code into the HTML area, and run it.

You can type in text (or any HTML) before or after the iFrame, and even change the size of the video by editing the width and height in the iFrame.

FORM

4

Sending Information

A YouTube video has "?watch=abcde" at the end of its URL. That's extra information. In this case, it's the video ID, being sent to the website so YouTube knows what to show you. When you submit a web form, that's one of the ways the information gets to the server so it can process it.

I'm an HTML tag in communication mode. When a user has to enter information on a website, it's me that allows them to do so. You know what I mean—websites where you have to enter text or check a box.

My "submit" button is critical! This is what lets the user send all the information they just entered back to Server for processing. Without me, you couldn't create an account, enter information, or even do a web search!

In the Know:

HTML Form tags let you enter and submit information, but they don't actually process it! Instead, all the data you enter is sent to the website's server, as part of the request for the next web page. The server processes the data and responds with the next page.

CSS

My full name is Cascading Style Sheets, but I prefer CSS. While HTML is good at deciding what goes on a web page, it will only ever give you the basics of styling a website. I bring a whole new level of pizzazz—why else would I use the <style> tag when working with HTML? That's my signal—it's a tag that tells Browser to switch from HTML to CSS. While HTML can do basic things such as bold type and line spacing, I'm much more powerful when it comes to looking good!

CSS DECLARATION

CSS sits right inside an HTML document, and it is my job to tell Browser which parts of the code are CSS and which are not. I do this by "declaring" CSS. Most of the time, I do this by using HTML's <style> and </style> tags. These tell Browser that everything between the tags is CSS.

Another method is to point to an external file, using the <link href=""> tag. In this case, the "href" part of the HTML code is simply a URL to a separate file that contains the CSS code. Another way, though not always the most efficient, is to add the "style=" attribute directly to an HTML element, using code that looks like this: <img style="width:100">. You can add a style attribute to almost any HTML element.

5

In the Know:

A "responsive" website changes depending on the device it's viewed on. Coders use CSS to change the style of an element based on the device's screen size. You can use CSS to show an image instead of a video on a phone, to add more spacing when it's on a laptop, or to change everything to green on a tablet—just go with your imagination!

White Space

As with HTML, CSS doesn't care about white space. As long as you have your syntax correct, it won't matter if you have gaps in your code!

CSS PROPERTY

I'm a formula that CSS uses to change Website's appearance. I usually start with a "selector." This tells Browser which HTML element(s) to apply this particular CSS to. Then I use a combination of colons (:), semicolons (;), and squiggly brackets { } to tell Browser all about my properties. There are so many things CSS can do using me: animate an attractive popup, for example; or make entire chunks of a page disappear; or keep a message onscreen while the user keeps scrolling. Oh, my talents are endless!

TRY THIS!

Here's a simple CSS example for JSFiddle. Type the following into the CSS area in JSFiddle. Note, you don't need <style> tags in JSFiddle!

b{ ·········· • called the selector, apply to all words with the b, or bold, HTML tag

color:green; ·········· • here's a property for color

font-size:14pt; ·········· • this sets the font size to 14 point

}

#boldone{ ·········· • the "#" means apply this to the single "boldone" element

    background-color:yellow; ······ • this sets the background color to yellow

    border:1px solid red; ·········· • this sets a border around the "boldone" element that is solid red and one pixel thick

}

Type the following into the HTML area of JSFiddle.

<p>Use CSS for <b id=boldone>one</b> or <b>all</b> elements! </p> ·····• the "id=boldone" is how the CSS #boldone selector knows which element to apply the style to

> Use CSS for `one` or **all** elements! ··········· • result looks like this

JAVASCRIPT

Ah, finally, you get to me, the brains of all website coding! Don't tell HTML and CSS, but I'm the smartest of the bunch by far! Unlike those guys, I can respond to what the user is doing. Then, using variables, loops, arrays, and anything else you can do with any other programming languages, I can control HTML and CSS and make them do what I want! It means I can change CSS styles, I can add HTML elements, and I can even send Browser to a completely different web page!

JAVASCRIPT DECLARATION

Like CSS, JavaScript hangs out inside HTML and I'm here to tell Browser when code is meant to be JavaScript instead of HTML. While CSS has a <style> tag, JavaScript uses a <script> tag. I slip this into the HTML header or, when using an external file, I use <script src="">.

There are a few ways to tell Browser when to run the JavaScript. One of the easiest is called "inline." That's where you put the JavaScript right inside the HTML—for example, <button onclick="runThisJavascript()">. You can guess that, in this case, when the user clicks the button, the "runThisJavascript()" code is called into action!

6

In the Know:

Don't confuse "Java" with JavaScript! Java is a very popular and complex programming language used by many businesses. It's also the language that Minecraft was originally coded in! Rumor has it that JavaScript got its name as a marketing gimmick in 1995 to sound like Java, a hot language at the time!

Language Libraries

Languages such as JavaScript have large sets of "libraries." They involve code that is prebuilt and boxed up ready for you to use to build something more complex. One library can be coded on top of another, giving quick and easy access to many things you might want to do in code. There are lots of JavaScript libraries available if you search online—for example, jQuery, which helps simplify JavaScript when working with HTML.

BASIC CODING

What would any programming language be without me—the basic coding language tools: variables, loops, functions, and conditions? Whatever language you use, you'll find me at its core.

Sure, JavaScript was invented to make web pages interactive and awesome, but deep down at that guy's heart, it's me that keeps things glued together with my standard programming tools. Need to store information like names? Declare a variable and I've got you covered. Want to repeat something, I've got loops for you. Yep! HTML and CSS don't support basic coding tools, but JavaScript does—as do most other programming languages.

6

Plain Talking

- **LOOP:** Repeats a section of code over and over again.

- **VARIABLE:** Stores a value or values that can be changed.

- **FUNCTION:** Sets a specific procedure or routine.

- **CONDITION:** Enables a program to react differently to sets of circumstances.

In the Know:

Every browser has a set of developer tools designed to help more advanced coders slice, dice, and analyze their code. On your browser, look for "Developer," "Developer Tools," or "Inspector" in the menu system, and you'll find cool tools for JavaScript!

TRY THIS!

Here's a short sample of what JavaScript looks like. Try it in JSFiddle by typing it into the JavaScript area!

```
for (i=1;i<=3;i++){
    alert ("Counting: " + i);
}
```

- loop three times, changing variable "i" from 1 to 3
- show a popup and count

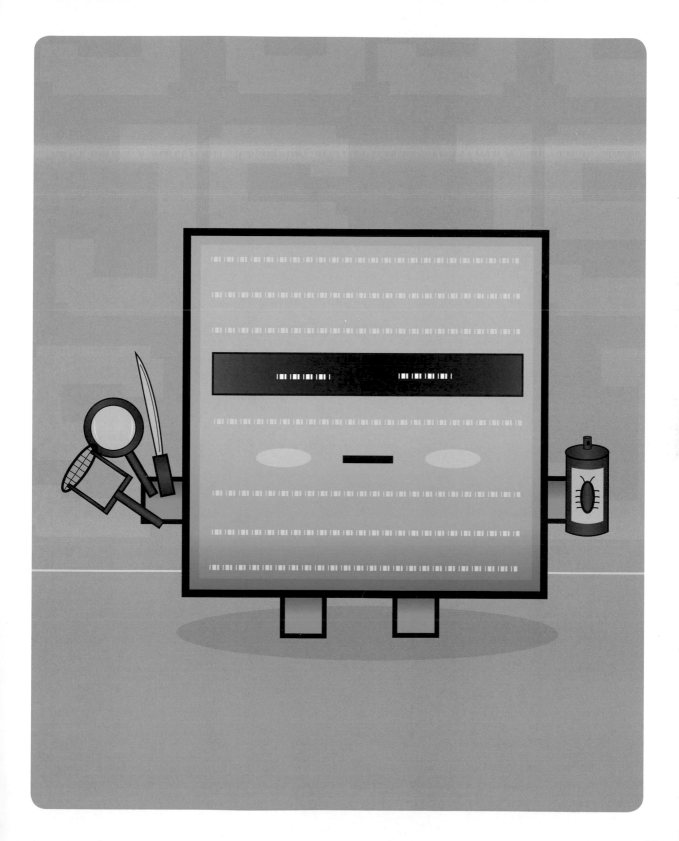

DOM

JavaScript would be pretty lifeless without me! Document Object Model is my full name. My job is to give JavaScript a means of finding and controlling any HTML element on the web page, and its CSS elements too.

Imagine giving JavaScript the power to change button colors, make images appear and disappear, or present popup messages in HTML. I work with Basic Coding to create loops, variables, and if/then statements that can make changes to a website on the fly. I can even check what the user's doing—for example, what field she's in, what she's typing, and even where her mouse pointer clicks!

6

TRY THIS!

Let's combine the three elements, and use DOM and JavaScript to change the CSS and HTML. Remember to type these into the appropriate areas in JSFiddle.

HTML

`<p>Some <b id="demo">red</b> text</p>` ·········· we gave some bold text an ID of "demo"

CSS

`b{color:red}` ·········· makes all bold text red

JAVASCRIPT

`alert ("ALERT! Color about to change!");`
`document.getElementById("demo").style.color = "green";` ·········· change text color
`document.getElementById("demo").innerHTML = "green";` ·········· change actual text

RESULT: Your screen should show red text, alert you the color is about to change, then change to green text.

DYNAMIC SERVER

When Basic Server sends a web page on Browser's request, that web page is usually "static." It is prewritten and always carries the same information—say, a store's address and opening times. Sometimes a server with more complex skills is needed—that's me! I create "dynamic" web pages on the fly, updating them with the latest data, such as game scores on a sports website. It means Website has extra setup and more complex code—oh, and me to handle it all!

SERVER-SIDE CODE

To build and return a dynamic web page, Dynamic Server needs instructions from me—programming that takes place at the server end of the browser–server system.

Unlike JavaScript, HTML, or CSS, which are read and run by Browser, my code is run on a server on the Internet. Remember, Browser's job is to show you the information, while a server is where all the information and content actually come from! It means that, whatever browser you're using—from wherever you are in the whole world—you can access the same information from the same, centrally located server, where code like me is running!

In the Know:

Server-side code can be written in a lot of different languages. PHP, Ruby, Go, and C#, are some examples of common server-side languages used by popular websites today, including Facebook, Google, and Twitter.

Handy Analogy

Here's one way to understand static vs dynamic pages. Imagine you are going on a field trip and you need a field-trip form. If your teacher (the server) hands you (the browser) a blank form to fill out, we'd call that a "static" page—it's the same exact page for all students. But if the teacher recognizes you and first writes your name and information for you before giving you the form, we call that a "dynamic" page—it's specific to you!

PHP

A special kind of Server-Side Code, I sit inside an HTML document with HTML, CSS, and JavaScript. I'm special, because my code is run by Dynamic Server. You'll recognize me by my opening tag of <?php and a closing tag of ?>. Say Browser requests a web page with the following contents:

Hello, the server time is currently
<?php print date("h:ia"); ?>.

Dynamic Server would first run the PHP statement, resulting in: Hello, the server time is currently 11:33am. It would then send the result back to Browser as if "11:33am" was part of the original file. It means Dynamic Server is able to supply Browser with the latest data every time.

Plain Talking

- **PHP:** Used to stand for Personal Home Page, but now stands for "PHP Hypertext Preprocessor."

In the Know:

PHP is the most popular language used today to build dynamic websites. It runs on a large number of dynamic websites. This means there's plenty of PHP knowledge out there, and a lot of support available through forums.

PHP Applications

A very powerful language, PHP can do many things—from reading and writing to creating a database to communicating with other Internet applications. It can only run on a server, so it can't directly interact with a user or control things like popups on a website.

DATABASE

Most modern websites need to store information: say, when they need to keep lists of usernames and passwords, or details of products and their descriptions, or anything else useful for tracking. All that information needs to be kept somewhere and it's my job to keep track of it.

I'm a clever tool that lets a computer store and find information superfast. Just think about how much data Amazon or Facebook has to keep. Amazon has more than 500 million products, while Facebook currently has well over two billion users! Finding information for one of those products or users in a split second isn't easy, but I'd like to say I'm pretty good at it.

7

In the Know:

The most popular computer language for operating a database is called SQL (pronounced "sequel"), which stands for Structured Query Language. It focuses on adding, updating, and reading data from tables, with command phrases such as "select-from" or "insert-into."

Database Administrator

Maintaining a database takes a lot of work! From making sure the data is written correctly, to getting hold of information as quickly as possible, it's a specialized skill. Many applications that use complex databases have a dedicated Database Administrator to help keep their data up to date and quick to access.

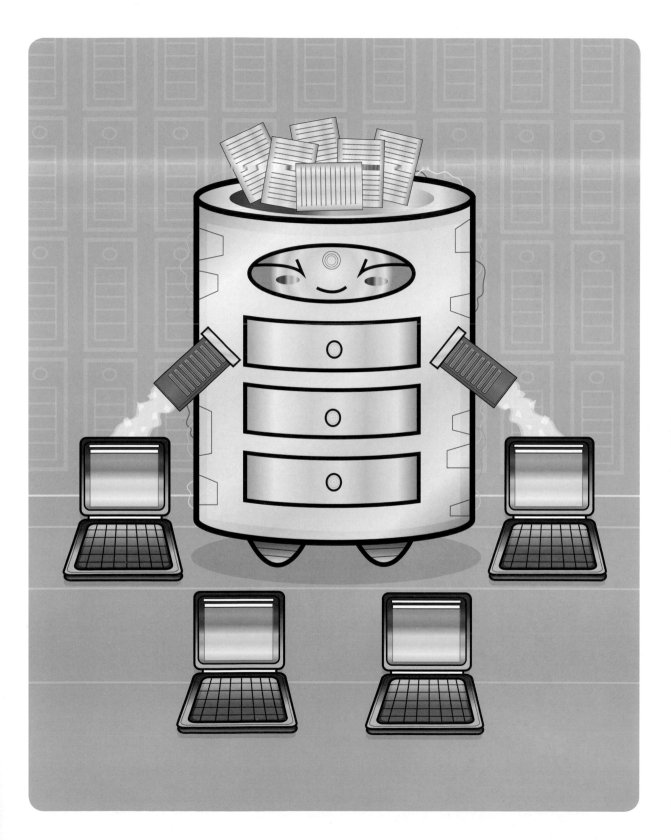

CODING A WEBSITE APP

Now that you've met the Dynamic Server crew, you're ready to create your own "dynamic" website! Simpler, static websites always show the same information, while a dynamic website allows you to input, store, and retrieve information. You'll be coding from files and using a real website host, accessible from any browser. Once you get the code working, you can try experimenting with it to do different things—that's the best way to understand code!

GETTING STARTED

8

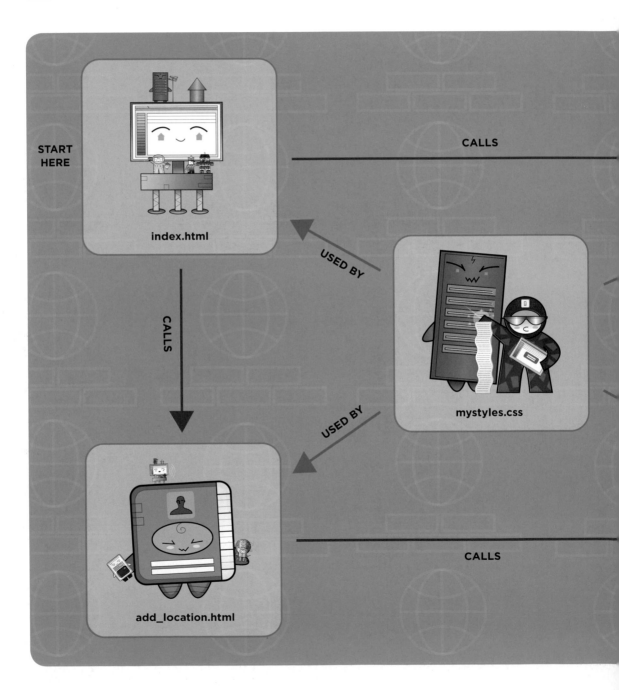

START HERE

index.html

CALLS

CALLS

USED BY

mystyles.css

USED BY

add_location.html

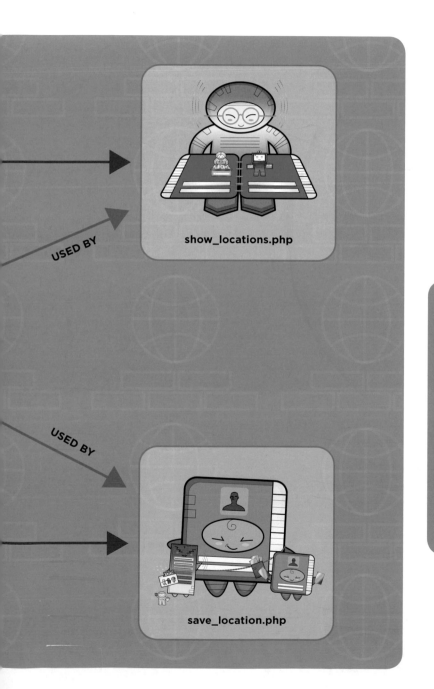

USED BY

show_locations.php

USED BY

save_location.php

You're going to build a super-simple dynamic web application that lets you create your very own list of favorite dessert shops with an address for each one. My diagram here gives an overview of the files and shows you how each element relates to the others. You'll find it handy to refer back to this diagram as you explore the code.

8

UPLOADING FILES TO THE WEBSITE HOST

To code from files like a pro, you need to sign up to a web-hosting platform. Remember, a web host is a computer on the Internet that provides a server for you to store your code files, and that responds to requests from browsers. There are plenty of options out there, from stable, paid hosts, such as GoDaddy or HostGator, to free, learning-oriented ones, such as 000webhostapp.com. You can choose whichever host you like, as long as it supports PHP. Also, on most hosting sites users must be 18 years or older. Please be sure to ask an adult to help you sign up for the account!

Caching

Sometimes you might upload your edited code only to find that it doesn't update on your site! This may be due to the "cache" (pronounced "cash"), which means the computer is using an old version it remembers, to make things faster. If this happens to you, try refreshing the browser page (Cmd R on a Mac) or using a different browser. Or if you're feeling adventurous, Google "hard refresh" for tips on how to force your browser to skip the cache.

DO THIS!

If you go on to edit your code or develop new projects, use a plain-text editor such as Notepad on a PC, or TextEdit on a Mac. Be sure to keep the exact same filename, and save files in a "plain-text format." The code won't run if you use Word or RTF.

Getting Started

Follow these steps to get your first web app running:

1 Create an account on a web host, such as 000webhost. To do that, go to www.000webhost.com, and follow the directions to sign up. You'll need an adult to help you create an account.

2 Download all five pre-built code files to your computer by going to **www.thecoderschool.com/ basher**, and following the directions there.

3 Once you've signed up and logged in to 000webhost, find the File Manager. Using the File Manager, upload all code files from Step 2 into your default folder (called public_html). Double-check the names of the files match ours exactly. If a filename doesn't match, simply rename it.

4 To test the application, open a browser and go to the URL assigned to you by 000webhost (for example "yourname.000webhostapp.com"). You should see a screen that says "Dessert Locations," as shown for index.html on page 86.

In the following pages, we'll take a closer look at each of the files you downloaded in Step 1. You can use this opportunity to experiment with the code. To change the code, edit the file on your computer, then use the File Manager to upload it again, and your app should be updated!

8

In the Know:

If you have any problems, you can always head to our site at www. thecoderschool.com/ basher and we'll see if we can troubleshoot them with you.

index.html

Your website starts with me. My name is used for the main page of many websites, not just yours. When Browser requests a domain name, such as www.website.com, it's my file name that Basic Server looks for. In my code, you can see where I provide links to the other guys in this chapter.

Dessert Locations

Let's make a list of your favorite local dessert shops. Click on the links below to get started!

Enter New location
See Locations

.......• screenshot of your web page

```
<!DOCTYPE HTML>
```
.......• indicates a standard html structure, as do the next two lines

```
<html>

<head>

    <title>Dessert Locations</title>
```
.......• title as it appears in the browser

```
    <link rel="stylesheet" type="text/css" href="mystyles.css" />
```
.......• refers to an external style sheet, in this case, mystyles.css (page 88)

```
</head>

<body style="background-color:gray">
```
.......• an inline style that makes the page background gray

```
<!-- This is a comment that the browser will ignore! -->

<div id="maindiv">
```
.......• "div" is used to format in CSS; note the "id," which corresponds to the "maindiv" ID in the mystyles.css file

```
    <h1>Dessert Locations</h1>

    <p>Let's make a lits of your favorite local Dessert Locations
```
.......• <p>indicates regular printed text and starts a new paragraph line

```
    <p>Click on the links below to get started!</p>

    <a href="add_location.html">Enter Dessert Location/a><br>
```
.......• <a> takes the user to a new file

```
    <a href="show_locations.php">See Dessert Locations/a>

</div>

</body>
```
.......• these are ending tags

```
</html>
```

mystyles.css

Whose styles? My styles! As you can see, I'm a CSS file. Everything inside me is CSS. Sometimes, inside an html file you need to declare CSS using <style></style>, but that's not the case with me. I'm a separate file altogether. When other files refer to me, Server knows to treat everything inside me as CSS. In your website, my role is to set the styles for the main part of all your web pages, where the ID of the <div> element is "maindiv."

8

```
#maindiv{ ............................................. all properties within the squiggly
                                                        brackets are for the div with an
                                                        ID of "maindiv"

    margin:auto; ..................................... centers the div

    width:50%; ...................................... uses half the width
                                                        of the window

    background-color:limegreen; ............. creates background color

    color:white; .................................... creates text color

    border-radius:20px; ........................... creates rounded corners

    border:2px solid black; ...................... creates a two-pixel-wide,
                                                        solid- black border

    padding:20px; .................................. adds some padding between
                                                        text and border.

    font-family:Verdana; ......................... sets the font as Verdana

    text-align:center; ............................. centers the text inside the div

}
```

add_location.
html

8

I deal with the part of your website that lets a user add new locations. I'm "called" from index.html, and my job is to use HTML's Form to let the user type in two things—the name of the dessert shop and its address. I also use a very simple JavaScript routine to raise an alert if the dessert shop name is blank by mistake. Once the user enters the info on my form, I package up whatever the user entered and send it onto my pal save_location.php.

Add a Dessert Shop

Dessert Shop Name: [_____]

Full Address (street, city, state): [_____]

[Submit]

screenshot of your web page.

```
<!DOCTYPE HTML>
<html>
<head>
    <title>Add a Dessert Shop</title>
    <link rel="stylesheet" type="text/css" href="mystyles.css" />
    <script>
    function validateForm() {
        if (document.getElementById('locationname').value == ""){
            alert ("Please enter a dessert shop name!");
            return false;
        } else {
        return true;
        }
    }
    </script>
</head>
<body>
<div id="maindiv">
    <h1>Add a Dessert Shop</h1>
    <form method="post" action="save_location.php" onsubmit="return validateForm()">
    <p>Dessert Shop Name: <input type=text name=locationname id=locationname></p>
    <p>Full Address (street, city, state): <input type=text name=address id=address></p>
    <input type=submit >
    </form>
    </div>
</body>
</html>
```

this JavaScript function is called when your form is submitted; it will return back a value of true if the form is valid, or false if it is not

use DOM (getElementById) to see if the value of dessert shop name is blank; notice two "=="— in many languages comparing values uses ==, while assigning a value is just one =

show pop-up to ask user to enter name

if we return false, then the page doesn't do anything; return true, and we'll send the user to save_location.php

else name is not blank, so return true

if you have data to send, use the form element; notice the "onsubmit" attribute—this tells the browser to run the validateForm() JavaScript function when the user submits this form

use an input tag to collect your data in a form

sends all input data inside the form element to the save_location.php page, as indicated by the earlier form tag; remember, in our case, because we have an onsubmit event, it will run the JavaScript first before moving on

8

save_
location.php

8

Now you've reached the part where you save some data! I take information passed to me by add_location.html and save it away to read later. My name ends with ".php," which means Server knows to read and run my PHP code before sending me over to Browser. Take a closer look at my code, and you'll see that I take the location info and write it to the end of a data file. That data file is used by show_locations.php to show you all the dessert shops you have entered.

In the Know:

What happens when you click "Submit"? It's complicated, but goes something like this: add_contact passes the new information over to save_contact. Then save_contact tucks it away in a form that might look strange to us but that makes sense to a computer. It mashes all that info (name, address, etc.) together. We call it serialization. When you want to see a contact, show_contacts reads the file and displays the ones you want.

Location saved! Go back <u>home</u>. ....• screenshot of your web page

```
<!DOCTYPE HTML>

<html>

<head>

    <title>Save Dessert Shop</title>

    <link rel="stylesheet" type="text/css" href="mystyles.css" />

</head>

<body style="background-color:gray">

<div id="maindiv">

<?php .........................................................•  everything inside the <?php
                                                                 and ?> brackets gets run by
                                                                 the server *before* sending the
                                                                 page shown above back to the
                                                                 browser

$newdata = implode ("|",$_POST); ...........................•  $_POST is a variable that
                                                                 contains all the input data sent
                                                                 by the calling page; in our case
                                                                 we'll find the dessert shop name
                                                                 and address in $_POST

file_put_contents("locationfile.txt", $newdata . "\n", FILE_APPEND); ....•  write the info from $_POST
                                                                 to the end of a file called
                                                                 "locationfile.txt

print "Dessert Shop saved! Go back <a href=index.html>home</a>.";
                                                              •  using "print" in PHP will write
                                                                 the text out as part of the file
                                                                 and send it back to the browser;
                                                                 this is the text that shows up in
                                                                 your screenshot, above

?>

</div>

</body>

</html>
```

show_ locations.php

In the Know:

Once you get all the code working, try editing it to let you enter different things. Here are some things you might try: instead of dessert shops, enter in your favorite movies and show the trailers. (Hint: replace the iframe line in this file with a Youtube video as shown by iFrame on page 56.) Or enter in your favorite bands with a link to their band webpage. (Hint: replace the iframe line with a link using <a href> as shown on page 53.) Once you really get the hang of it, the sky's the limit!

I'm here to show you the dessert shops that have been entered. My code uses PHP to read the locations that save_location.html wrote down, line by line. See how I use HTML's Table Tag to organize the list of locations. I also use HTML's iframe to show the user the location's address on a Google map! Once I build all the HTML code from the locations in a data file, Server sends it back to Browser to show a list of dessert shops, along with little Google maps of their addresses!

.... • screenshot of your web page.

(For brevity, we've omitted the initial HTML portion of this file.)

```php
<?php

if (file_exists("locationfile.txt")) {

    print "<table>";

    print "<tr><th>Dessert Shop</th><th>Map</th></tr>";

    $file = fopen("locationfile.txt","r");

    $data = fgets($file);

    while($data != "") {

        $fields = explode("|",$data);

        print "<tr>";

        print "<td>$fields[0]</td>"

        $address = urlencode($fields[1]);

        print "<td><iframe src=\"https://maps.google.com/maps?q=$address&output=embed\"></iframe></td>";

        print "</tr>";

        $data = fgets($file);

    }

    print "</table>";

    fclose($file);

} else {

    print "Sorry, no locations yet.";

}

?>
```

locationfile.txt is where we saved our locations; first check to see if we have that file—if not, it means there aren't any locations yet

print table and the header row; printing means it's output as part of the file—in this case, as HTML

first, open the file for reading

read one line

keep reading the file line by line until the line is empty

in save_location.php we built a string of text to save to the file; this reads that string and breaks it up into name and address

start the row in HTML

once broken out, $fields[0] is the name and $fields[1] is the address

Google requires a certain format, which urlencode helps support

this is the HTML code that uses Google to show each map

end of table row

read next line in the file

end the table

close the data file when we're done

this "else" is from checking if the file exists on our first PHP line above, so if file does NOT exist, there are no locations yet

8

INDEX

Page numbers in **bold** are
main entries